# The Lamp Lighter

# The Lamp Lighter

A Practice of Intentional Light

Jo Landolfo

Intentional Light Publishing

Published by Intentional Light Publishing

First Edition, 2026

ISBN: 979-8-9943858-3-8

Printed in the United States of America

This book is intended for inspirational and educational purposes only and does not replace professional medical, psychological, legal, or financial advice. Always seek qualified professionals for matters concerning your health, safety, or well-being.

# Contents

Introduction — The Nomad Within ........ 1
We Are All Travelers ........ 3
The Question of Destination ........ 3
Manifesting isn't magic. It's direction. ........ 5
Why Definition Matters ........ 5
Vision: Giving the Mind a Map ........ 5
Use the Senses ........ 6
Getting Lost and Finding the Way ........ 7
The Road You Walk ........ 9
PART I — DEFINITIONS: NAMING THE LIGHT ........ 11
What Is Intentional Light ........ 11
What It Is Not ........ 14
Faith as a Choice ........ 15
The Meaning of a Lamp Lighter ........ 16
What It Looks Like in Real Life ........ 17
How This Applies to Your Life ........ 17
Light, Flame, and Carrying ........ 18
Carrying It for Yourself ........ 18
Carrying It for Others ........ 19
Everyday Examples ........ 19

The Quiet Truth ........ 21

PART II – IDENTIFICATION: SEEING THE LIGHT ........ 23

Noticing What Has Always Been There ........ 23

How Light Shows Up in Ordinary Life ........ 24

The Gift of Contrast ........ 26

When You Dim Yourself ........ 27

When You Light Yourself ........ 29

Recognizing Lamp Lighters ........ 31

Learning From the Dark Without Living There ........ 33

PART III – VALIDATION: TRUSTING WHAT YOU KNOW ........ 35

Why You Learned to Doubt Yourself ........ 35

Fear Versus Intuition ........ 36

The Body Knows First ........ 38

Quiet Knowing ........ 39

Reclaiming Inner Authority ........ 40

Letting Your Light Count ........ 40

Trusting the Road Beneath You ........ 41

PART IV – APPLICATION: BECOMING A LAMP LIGHTER ........ 43

Lighting Yourself First ........ 43

Boundaries as Flame Protection ........ 43

Rest as Fuel ........ 44

Calm as Strength ........ 46

Presence as Medicine ........ 46
Lighting Without Burning Out ........ 47
Walking Away Without Going Dark ........ 48
Becoming What You Needed ........ 49
CLOSING – CARRYING THE LIGHT FORWARD ........ 50
You Don't Save the World ........ 50
You Tend the Flame ........ 50
Others Find You by It ........ 51
Acknowledgments ........ 52
About the Author ........ 53

# Introduction — The Nomad Within

In a way, we are all nomads in life. Not because we move from place to place, but because nothing inside us stays the same forever. We travel through seasons of becoming. Through love and loss. Through certainty and doubt. Through versions of ourselves we once thought were permanent. Some of us walk steady roads. Some of us wander. Some of us get lost more than once. And maybe that's not failure. Maybe that's the work. Because sometimes, if you don't get lost, you never learn how to find the way. Being lost teaches you to listen. To notice. To trust what doesn't shout. Getting lost isn't a failure of direction. It's part of becoming. Some people get lost early. Some get lost after they think they were found. You can get lost: When you're young and making choices with half a map. When something breaks that you thought was permanent. When a dream works, but not the way you thought it would. When love changes shape. When success doesn't feel like home. We're taught that getting lost means you messed up. But most people who grow didn't grow in straight lines. You can get lost at:

- Sixteen
- Thirty
- Fifty
- Seventy

It doesn't check your age before it shows up. Trauma can knock you off the road.

So can joy. Marriage.

- Graduation.
- A new job.

- A diagnosis.
- A death.
- A birth.
- A single sentence that changes everything.

Life can turn in a New York minute—and suddenly the road you were walking disappears. Being lost feels like:

- Standing in a place that doesn't match your map
- Carrying a name that doesn't fit anymore
- Living a life you didn't mean to arrive in

But here's the quiet truth:

- You don't get lost because you're weak.
- You get lost because you're alive.

Getting lost strips away what was borrowed. It asks what is actually yours. It teaches you to read signs you ignored before.

And sometimes—the road you were on has to end so the road that is yours can begin.
I lived that truth in my own journey, and it carried me into nearly a decade on the road, traveling across this country alone.
I learned who I was when there was no script, no familiar map—just me, my choices, and the miles ahead.

This book isn't about highways and campgrounds.
It's about the road you walk inside your own life.
The path only you can choose.
The light you carry when maps fail.

You don't need to see the whole journey.
You only need enough light to take the next step.

# We Are All Travelers

Most people don't wake up one day and think, "Ah yes, I am a traveler in life." They realize it when something moves that they thought was fixed.

You notice you're a traveler when:

- A role you lived inside disappears
- A dream changes shape
- A person you counted on is gone
- A version of you no longer fits

Stillness teaches very little. Movement teaches everything. When Do You Realize You're Traveling?

You realize when:

- You grieve something you can't return to
- You outgrow something you once begged for
- You arrive somewhere that doesn't feel like "home"
- You feel between lives instead of inside one

That's when you feel it: "I am not parked. I am passing through."

# The Question of Destination

Everyone asks it differently:

- "What am I headed toward?"
- "What am I supposed to become?"
- "What is the point of all this moving?"

People say words like:

- Peace
- Love
- Happiness
- Security

But those are umbrellas. Not addresses.

- One person's peace is another person's prison.
- One person's love is another person's loss.
- One person's security is another person's cage.

That's why defining your destination is hard, you can't borrow it from someone else.

Your Insight Is Dead-On when you learn something real:

- Manifesting doesn't work with fog.
- It needs shape.
- "Peace" is vague.

But:

- Peace might mean waking without dread
- Peace might mean having your own space
- Peace might mean not being afraid to speak

"Happiness" is vague.

But:

- Happiness might mean creating
- Happiness might mean being useful
- Happiness might mean being free

You don't choose a destination by copying a word.

You choose it by describing a life you would recognize.

Maybe the Real Destination Isn't a place.

It's a state of being you can name clearly enough to walk toward:

- Who you are allowed to be
- How you are allowed to feel
- What you are no longer willing to trade yourself for

The clearer you get, the easier the road becomes to read.

## Manifesting isn't magic. It's direction.

You don't get what you "wish" for.
You move toward what you can see.

### Why Definition Matters

A vague destination creates wandering.
A clear one creates movement.

"Peace" doesn't tell your feet where to go.
But:

- "Waking without dread" does.
- "Having my own space" does.
- "Living without shrinking" does.

Manifesting begins when you stop speaking in clouds
and start speaking in coordinates.

### Vision: Giving the Mind a Map

A vision board—physical or mental—is not decoration.
It's rehearsal.

It works because your mind learns by exposure:

- What you look at often feels familiar
- What feels familiar feels possible

When you build a vision, don't just show:

- What you want
  But:
- How it feels to live there

## Use the Senses

If it's real, it has texture.

Ask:

- What do I see when I wake up?
- What do I hear in this life?
- What do I touch often?
- What does my body feel like here—tense or free?
- What emotions show up most days?

You're not designing a dream.
You're designing a lived day.

**Writing It Into Your Life**

Reading can open a door.
Writing is how you walk through it.

Journaling turns vision into ownership.

When you write:
• You slow down
• You get honest
• You notice contradictions
• You correct course

Writing is how a vision moves from fantasy into identity.
You stop saying:
"I want a life like this."
And start saying:
"This is the life I am building."

That's when the traveler stops wandering
and starts walking on purpose.

The companion journal, The **Solo Woman Traveler's Survival Journal,** exists for this reason—to give your inner road a place to speak.

# Getting Lost and Finding the Way

Being lost is uncomfortable because it threatens the story you're telling yourself about where you're going.

Most people don't hate being lost because of confusion.
They hate it because it suggests they might have to change.

Some never realize they're lost.
They just keep walking in a direction that no longer belongs to them—
busy, tired, numb, productive, responsible… and quietly empty.

But the body knows before the mind admits it.

Intuition doesn't usually scream.
It whispers.

At first, the signs are small:

- Restlessness you can't explain
- A dull dissatisfaction you keep ignoring

- A sense that something is "off," but not broken enough to fix
- Success that doesn't feel like home

It's like seeing a storm far away.
The sky still looks fine where you're standing,
but the air feels different.

The signposts start to look wrong.
Not broken—just not meant for you anymore.

You tell yourself:
"It's probably nothing."
"I should be grateful."
"I'll deal with it later."

But intuition keeps tapping.

Awareness is the first real step.
Not action.
Not change.

Just honesty.

"I am not where I thought I would be."
"This road doesn't feel like mine."
"I am not broken—but I am not aligned."

Listening doesn't mean burning your life down.
It means turning your head toward the whisper
instead of pretending you didn't hear it.

That's how the traveler begins again—
not with certainty,
but with attention.

# The Road You Walk

Choosing the road matters because not every road leads where you actually want to go.

Once you define your destination clearly,
a lot of confusion disappears.

Some options stop making sense.
Some temptations lose their shine.
Some doors quietly close themselves.

Clarity is a filter.

But clarity alone isn't enough.
You also need honesty.

Critical thinking is what keeps a dream from becoming a fantasy.
It asks:

- What is actually possible for me?
- What is in my control?
- What will cost more than I'm willing to pay?

Realism isn't pessimism.
It's respect for reality.

A destination without a path is just a wish.

That's where breaking it down matters.

Big visions overwhelm the nervous system.
Small steps calm it.

"How do you eat an elephant? One bite at a time."
Not glamorous—but true.

You don't build a life in one leap.
You build it in:

- Decisions
- Habits
- Adjustments
- Course corrections

Each step is a choice to stay on your road.

You don't need to see the whole journey.
You just need to know:
"This step belongs to the life I am choosing."

# PART I — DEFINITIONS: NAMING THE LIGHT

## What Is Intentional Light

Intentional Light isn't one thing.
It's a way of choosing.

Every person will see it through their own lens—
religion, philosophy, trauma, culture, science, faith, doubt.

They're all touching different parts of the same elephant.

Some people need structure.
Some need mystery.
Some need proof.
Some need poetry.

And some cling tightly to one definition because it feels like safety.

The danger isn't belief.
The danger is insisting that only one doorway exists.

We don't all fit in the same box.
We don't all need the same language.
But we all need meaning that works in our own lives.

That's why Intentional Light has to be defined personally.

Not as a doctrine.
Not as a rulebook.

But as:

- What lifts you instead of shrinks you
- What steadies you instead of scares you
- What helps you show up better, not smaller

If it inspires you,
if it gives you courage,
if it fits your life instead of fighting it,
then it belongs to you.

This book isn't here to convert.
It's here to invite.

The language must be safe enough for the cautious
and wide enough for the curious.

Not threatening.
Not demanding.
Just offering light in many forms
and letting each person choose how to carry it.

In the real world, Intentional Light already exists under a hundred different names. People are practicing it every day—they just don't all call it the same thing.

Here are some of the ways it shows up:

In religion, it might be called:

- God's will
- Grace
- Walking in the Spirit
- Dharma
- Allah's guidance
- The path of righteousness
- Living in faith

In spirituality, it might be:

- Higher self
- Inner light
- Source
- Universal energy
- Awakening
- Conscious living
- Alignment

In philosophy, it might be:

- Virtue
- The good life
- Moral clarity
- Stoic calm
- Right action
- Human dignity

In psychology and self-work, it might be:

- Emotional intelligence
- Self-awareness
- Healing
- Integration
- Growth mindset
- Trauma recovery
- Self-trust

In everyday language, people call it:

- Doing the right thing
- Following your gut
- Being true to yourself
- Living with purpose
- Having a good heart
- Staying grounded
- Keeping your head on straight

Different names.
Same impulse.

To choose awareness instead of sleepwalking.
To choose kindness without losing strength.
To choose truth without cruelty.
To choose direction instead of drift.

That's Intentional Light—
whatever name someone gives it,
as long as it helps them walk their road with more honesty, courage, and care.

# What It Is Not

Intentional Light isn't a belief you hold.

It's a way you move.

You don't *have* it.
You *practice* it.

That's why it's more a verb than a noun.

It shows up in:

- What you notice
- What you ignore
- What you allow
- What you walk away from
- What you protect

Talking about light is easy.
Living by it is work.

It means:

- Checking in with yourself often
- Adjusting when you drift

- Choosing again when you forget
- Staying awake instead of comfortable

It's not a mood.
It's not a phase.
It's not something you post and move on from.

It's awareness kept active.
Presence kept sharp.
Choice kept alive.

You don't practice Intentional Light once.
You practice it daily—
sometimes hourly—
sometimes in the middle of a hard moment
when no one else sees what you choose.

That's where it becomes real.

# Faith as a Choice

You will know when you have faith that actually lasts—chosen, not inherited.

You didn't swallow a story because someone told you to.
You tested it.
You read.
You questioned.
You watched what happened when you walked that way.

And what convinced you wasn't theory.
It was a result.

When your thinking softened,
when your reactions calmed,

when your days felt steadier,
that was the proof.

Faith didn't arrive like lightning.
It arrived like pavement.

Smoother.
More predictable.
Less punishing.

Not perfect—just kinder to walk on.

You didn't wake up transformed.
You noticed that:

- The potholes were fewer
- The crashes were rarer
- The detours weren't as brutal

That's how a path earns trust.

Not by promises.
But by how it treats your feet.

# The Meaning of a Lamp Lighter

Being a Lamp Lighter isn't about being wise, perfect, or ahead.
It's about how you stand next to someone who's trying to see.

A Lamp Lighter does not say, "This is the way."
They say, "You have a way. Let's help you see it."

You became one the moment you stopped needing people to copy you
and started wanting them to trust themselves.

## What It Looks Like in Real Life

When someone is hurting, a Lamp Lighter doesn't rush in with answers.
They sit.
They listen.
They say, "Tell me what feels off."

They don't fix.
They help someone hear their own knowing.

When someone is confused, a Lamp Lighter doesn't give directions.
They ask better questions:

- What do you already know but haven't said out loud?
- What feels heavy?
- What feels like relief?

They don't carry someone else's pack.
They help them learn how to carry their own.

## How This Applies to Your Life

You practice being a Lamp Lighter when:

- You stop rescuing and start respecting
- You stop directing and start witnessing
- You stop needing to be right and start being present

In your own life:

- You don't force clarity—you wait for it
- You don't betray your knowing to make others comfortable
- You choose honesty over approval

You light your own lamp by:

- Listening to your body

- Trusting your quiet yes and no
- Walking away from what dims you

And when others see that, something happens.

They don't copy your life.
They recognize their own.

That's how light spreads—
not by telling,
but by showing what is possible when someone trusts themselves.

# Light, Flame, and Carrying

Carrying the light isn't dramatic.
It's ordinary—and that's why it works.

It's not speeches.
It's behaviors.

## Carrying It for Yourself

You carry your flame when:

- You pause instead of reacting.
- Even when you're triggered, you breathe first,
- You tell yourself the truth.
- Not the comfortable version—the honest one.
- You leave what dims you
- Even when it would be easier to stay.
- You protect your energy
- You stop over-explaining.
- You stop proving.
- You rest without guilt.

- You listen to your body.
- You notice when it tightens, shuts down, or relaxes.

That's you keeping your lamp lit.

## Carrying It for Others

You don't shine at people.
You walk near them.

You carry light when:

- You don't rush someone's grief
- You don't minimize someone's fear
- You don't hijack someone's story with your own
- You don't tell them what they "should" feel

Instead, you say:

- "I'm here."
- "You're not wrong to feel this."
- "Take your time."

That alone is light.

## Everyday Examples

At work:
Someone is overwhelmed.
You don't criticize—you steady the room.
Your calm becomes permission.

In family:
Someone is stuck.
You don't rescue—you remind them they can choose.

In friendship:
Someone doubts themselves.
You don't fix—you reflect what you already see in them.

In conflict:
You don't try to win.
You try to understand.

The deepest way I ever became a Lamp Lighter was when I cared for my daughter, and later, when she entered hospice.

It was the hardest thing I have ever done.
And somehow, the most meaningful.

I didn't try to fix what couldn't be fixed.
I didn't pretend everything would be okay.

I chose acceptance over fear.
Presence over panic.
Love over denial.

I held space so she could feel safe.
I carried calm so she wouldn't have to carry fear.

I like to believe that her transition was gentler because of that.
And I know my grief was softer because I did not abandon her—or myself—in that moment.

Being a Lamp Lighter isn't about brightness.
It's about staying when the dark is real
and choosing love anyway.

# The Quiet Truth

Light isn't loud.
It doesn't argue.
It doesn't demand.

It just makes the next step easier to see.

# PART II — IDENTIFICATION: SEEING THE LIGHT

## Noticing What Has Always Been There

"Can't see the trees for the forest" is exactly it. Life gets loud, busy, demanding, and before you know it you're running on noise instead of noticing.

Most people don't change when they're uncomfortable.
They change when something breaks.

A flat tire.
A breakdown.
A diagnosis.
A loss.
A collapse of something they thought was solid.

Before that, the rule is usually:
"If it's not broken, don't fix it."

But some things aren't broken—they're just headed there.

You don't always see the cliff when you're moving fast.
You don't hear the river until you're close enough to fall in.

That's why reflection matters before crisis.

Light isn't just for emergencies.
It's for maintenance.

When you practice awareness regularly:

- You notice fatigue before burnout

- You notice resentment before bitterness
- You notice fear before collapse
- You notice misalignment before disaster

Reflection is like pulling over before the engine smokes.

You don't wait for the crash to check the road.
You look ahead while you still have room to turn.

Becoming filled with light before you need it means:

- You're steadier when something shakes you
- You're clearer when something scares you
- You're calmer when something breaks

Then redirection doesn't feel like panic.
It feels like wisdom arriving on time.

The truth is the Light; the Intentional Light has always been there within you.

# How Light Shows Up in Ordinary Life

Your life doesn't have to be dramatic or extraordinary to matter. My life did include moments of deep breaking—moments that forced me to turn inward and search my own soul. That was my road. It does not have to be yours.

I became a Lamp Lighter for myself first, and then for others, because I lived the work. Not because I read about it. Not because someone handed me a map. Because I walked through darkness and learned how to carry my own light out.

I will tell you honestly—there were moments when I wished someone had stood in my life earlier, holding a small steady flame, showing me that another way was possible. I had regrets. Many of them. But my faith taught me something deeper than regret:

There is no right age.
No correct moment.
No universal event that wakes everyone up.

There is only now.

The past cannot be changed.
The future never arrives—it is always imagined.
Life only ever happens in this moment you are standing in.

People meet Light in different ways.
Some through quiet awakenings—books, conversations, simple realizations.
Some through earthquakes—loss, illness, collapse, reckoning.

Some recognize the light and turn toward it.
Some see it and choose the dark, because it feels familiar.

Light does not force itself.
It invites.

I do not carry light to save you.
I carry it so you can see what is possible.

If you look up and notice my flame,
and something in you thinks,
"I could carry my own," then this journey is already working.

# The Gift of Contrast

Self-awareness is not something you hold perfectly all the time.
Sometimes it's a long practice.
Sometimes it's a single clear moment. Contrast is what lets you see.

Without contrast, everything blends.
Without contrast, you don't notice light because there is nothing to compare it to.

Life teaches through difference:

- Calm is known because you've felt chaos.
- Safety is known because you've felt fear.
- Truth is known because you've lived in confusion.

Contrast sharpens perception.

- When you pause—even briefly—and notice:
  "This feels heavy,"
  "This feels peaceful,"
  "This drains me,"
  "This restores me,"
  you are learning through contrast.

Most people live in blur:
Not bad enough to change.
Not good enough to feel free.
Just gray.

But awareness brings colors back.

You begin to see:

- What is nourishing
- What is numbing
- What is yours

- What you've been carrying that never belonged to you

Contrast breaks the lie that life is only black or white, right or wrong, win or lose.
It shows you that most of life is choice in motion.

Sometimes awareness only lasts a moment:
A breath.
A realization.
A quiet "no" inside your chest.

That moment matters.

Because once you see contrast, you cannot unsee it.
You may still choose the hard road—but now you know you are choosing.
You may still stay—but you know what staying costs.

Contrast gives you sight.
Sight gives you choice.
And choice is the beginning of freedom.

# When You Dim Yourself

You don't always dim yourself because you are weak.
Sometimes you dim because you are tired.

For me, it happened most in moments of low energy—
when doubt felt louder than truth,
and my ego decided it had a microphone.

That ego voice is not wise.
It is loud.

It is dramatic.
It sides easily with darkness.

A real drama mama.

It doesn't speak gently.
It interrupts.
It exaggerates.
It tells stories that sound urgent but feel wrong.

Over time, I learned something important:

I didn't have to obey that voice.

I learned to:

- Hear it
- Acknowledge it
- And not follow it

I didn't always hear words.
But I felt the message:

"You're not enough."
"You're wrong."
"You should hide."
"You should shrink."

And instead of arguing, I practiced something quieter:

I listened…
and then I chose differently.

I learned to notice:

- When my energy was low
- When my patience was thin
- When fear was borrowing my voice

That's when ego gets bold.

Light doesn't shout.
It doesn't compete.
It waits.

So now, when that loud voice shows up,
I don't wrestle it.

I say, quietly inside:
"I hear you. But you're not in charge."

And I turn back toward what feels steady, honest, and calm.

That is how I stop dimming myself—
not by silencing the ego,
but by choosing not to let it lead.

# When You Light Yourself

Real change didn't happen the moment I realized I needed light.
Knowing and becoming are not the same thing.

It took time.
It took repetition.
It took reminding myself that the old thoughts and patterns
were no longer working.

At first, nothing looked dramatic.
There were no fireworks.
Just small shifts.

I noticed:

- I paused before reacting
- I listened before defending
- I breathed before deciding

I was building new patterns the way you build muscle—slowly, by using it again and again.

Faith within faith.

Not just believing in light,
but believing I could live by it.

The changes were subtle at first.
But I could feel them.

I noticed:

- My reactions softened
- My thoughts slowed
- My choices felt calmer

I was no longer living in knee-jerk moments.
Mindful thinking began to replace confusion.

And then one day, I realized something quietly amazing:

I was aware of my awareness.

I could see myself choosing.
I could feel myself pausing.
I could notice the space between impulse and action.

That space—that breath—that pause—
was my light showing up.

That was the moment I knew:

I wasn't just talking about Intentional Light anymore.
I was living it.

# Recognizing Lamp Lighters

As my own light grew steadier, I began to notice it in others.
Some people carried it quietly.
Some people carried it loudly.
And some only said they carried it.

That's when it got confusing.

I saw people who spoke beautifully about light, love, truth, and awakening—
but their presence felt sharp, heavy, performative.
Their words lifted them above others instead of beside them.

It unsettled me.

I wondered:
Am I being judgmental?
Or am I seeing something real?

That question became its own lesson.

Because real light doesn't need applause.
It doesn't posture.
It doesn't prove.
It doesn't announce itself.

Truth in the Light feels:

- Calm
- Grounded
- Spacious

- Safe

Ego-light feels:

- Loud
- Urgent
- Defensive
- Hungry for recognition

One soothes the room.
The other feeds on it.

At first, I reacted with irritation.
Then with doubt.
Then with silence.

Over time, I learned a softer response.

I didn't have to expose.
I didn't have to confront.
I didn't have to compete.

I only had to notice.

Light teaches you what to follow—
and just as clearly, what not to.

Without anger.
Without superiority.
Without war.

I learned to say inside:
"This is not my road."

Not as a verdict.
As a direction.

And I learned something else:

Seeing clearly does not require judging harshly.
It only requires honesty.

Real light feels peaceful.
Not impressive.
Not dramatic.
Not loud.

When something is true,
it doesn't need to shout.

And when I feel that quiet knowing in my body—
steady, calm, clear—
I trust it.

That is how I walk past what isn't mine
without turning it into a fight.

# Learning From the Dark Without Living There

Darkness is not the enemy.
It is the contrast that teaches you what light is.

Without up, there is no down.
Without wrong, you don't recognize right.
Without pain, you don't understand peace.

Darkness gives shape to meaning.

But learning from it is not the same as staying in it.

Recognizing and acknowledging a dark season
does not mean you make it your home.

It means you visit it long enough to understand:

- What it taught you
- What it cost you
- What you will not repeat

Darkness says:
"This hurt."
"This didn't work."
"This is not who I want to be again."

Wallowing is when you keep rehearsing the pain
instead of releasing its lesson.

Learning is when you say:
"I see what happened.
I know what it showed me.
And I am choosing differently now."

Sometimes the dark is in your past.
Sometimes it's just a dim stretch of road you're walking now.

Either way, the work is the same:

- Notice
- Name
- Learn
- Turn

You don't deny the dark.
You don't glorify it.
You don't live there.

You thank it for the lesson
and keep walking toward light.

# PART III — VALIDATION: TRUSTING WHAT YOU KNOW

## Why You Learned to Doubt Yourself

Doubting yourself doesn't usually come from one moment.
It comes from a lifetime of shaping. Family. School. Religion.
Culture. Relationships. Praise. Criticism or Silence.

All of it teaches you, quietly, what you are allowed to be, feel, and want.

I can't point to the exact day I learned to doubt myself.
I just know there was a time when living that way stopped working.

Something in me knew:
This is not the life I was meant to live.
This way of thinking is costing me more than it gives.

As you've seen throughout these pages, the path back is not a formula.
It is personal.
Slow.
Uneven.

Some people can name the moment they changed.
Some cannot.

And maybe that answer doesn't matter.

What matters is now.

Now is where choice lives.
Now is where patterns can be interrupted.
Now is where new thoughts can be practiced.

You may never fully understand every reason you learned to doubt yourself.
You don't need to.

You only need to notice when doubt no longer serves you.
When it no longer protects you.
When it no longer tells the truth.

Change begins when you are willing to say:

"This thought is not helping me."
"This pattern is not who I want to be."
"This voice is not my truth."

You don't erase a lifetime overnight.
You replace it moment by moment.

Every time you choose a kinder thought,
a truer response,
a calmer action,
you are rewriting what once wrote you.

Not by force.
By practice.

# Fear Versus Intuition

Discerning fear from intuition was a line I learned to walk slowly, because both had served me before.
I realized I didn't need to choose one. I needed to understand both.

Fear and darkness warned me of possible danger—the fight, the need for flight, the moment to freeze.
I reacted quickly, sometimes without being able to name the threat.
My body knew before my mind did.

But intuition is different.
It isn't loud.
It doesn't rush.
It doesn't scare me into motion.

Intuition is a knowing.
An awareness.
A calm whisper that suggests a direction.

Fear protects.
Intuition guides.

One alerts you to danger.
The other shows you where the light is.

One day I was driving down I-25.
Traffic was heavy, impatient, fast.

And then a feeling came over me—
slow down.

It wasn't loud.
It wasn't dramatic.
Just a small knowing that grew stronger with every second.

I listened.
I slowed—right as I crested the hill.

Without warning, traffic ahead was at a dead standstill.
No signs.
No flares.
No time to think.

An eighteen-wheeler was behind me.
Because I had already slowed, I had space.
I stopped in time.
I eased slightly to the right so the trucker had room to brake.

There was no pileup.
No chaos.
Just a long breath of relief we all seemed to take at once.

Miles later, the trucker passed me and gave me a thumbs-up.

We had both slowed—
even before we knew why.

That's how intuition speaks.
Not with fear.
Not with noise.

With timing.

# The Body Knows First

I feel fear in my body before I ever name it in my mind.
It moves through me like a chemical storm—
heat, speed, tension, electricity.

Fear has a mind of its own.
Sometimes it creeps in slow.
Sometimes it explodes without warning.

My reactions turn sharp.
My energy spikes.
My body prepares to fight, flee, or freeze.

And when the danger passes, my body tells the truth.
I shake.
I collapse.
I go quiet.

Intuition is nothing like that.

Intuition is gentle awareness.
It doesn't hijack me.
It invites me.

Sometimes it's a whisper.
Sometimes it becomes a nag.

"Listen to me," it says—not in panic,
but in persistence.

It repeats itself
not to scare me,
but to keep me from forgetting what I already know.

# Quiet Knowing

Familiarity, built through steady self-awareness, teaches you to recognize the quiet knowing.
The more you understand yourself, the easier it becomes to hear what is true.

The Light is in the details—
the small signals,
the subtle shifts,
the moments you choose to notice.

Those details are what fuel your Lamp.

# Reclaiming Inner Authority

Reclaiming inner authority only works because it was always yours to begin with.
You aren't creating it.
You're remembering it.

The ego has always had a problem with that kind of awareness.
It hates being seen clearly.

That's when it starts yelling:
shoulda,
coulda,
woulda—

like a schoolyard bully that doesn't build anything,
only tries to steal your lunch money and call it power.

But real authority doesn't shout.
It doesn't shame.
It doesn't replay old tapes.

It stands.
It knows.

# Letting Your Light Count

I don't always know how to measure my light.
Maybe it counts as gratitude—
that even when a door slammed shut,
I still found my way to a place that was right for me,
even when I couldn't understand it at the time.

I didn't have clarity.
I had movement.

I didn't have proof.
I had trust.

Maybe that's what faith really is—
not knowing where you're going,
but knowing you are still being guided.

That's not weakness.
That's courage without applause.

# Trusting the Road Beneath You

I trust the road beneath me because it is being paved with the things
I truly wanted in my life.
I know that because of where I stand right now.

My choices feel wiser.
My patience comforts me.
My awareness lights the path of choice.
And my journey points the direction.

# PART IV — APPLICATION: BECOMING A LAMP LIGHTER

## Lighting Yourself First

The first thing you're taught on an airplane is this:
when the oxygen mask drops, you put it on yourself first.

Not because you're selfish—
but because you can't help anyone if you're unconscious.

Poor choices come from living unaware.
From moving through life half-asleep.

I can't walk a path in darkness.
I have to light the way so I can see my choices,
and choose them on purpose.

## Boundaries as Flame Protection

This is one of the hardest things most of us ever learn.
We were raised to believe that boundaries are selfish.
That love means giving until it hurts—or you don't care.

But boundaries exist because we *do* care.
For ourselves.
For others.

They don't have to be a fortress.
They don't need a moat.
They just need to be clear.

Allowing people to make their own choices is vital for everyone's growth.
Control isn't love.
Rescue isn't always kindness.

Ego has a lot to say about this.
Ego says you're abandoning someone.
Ego says you're hiding.
Ego says you're cruel for choosing yourself.

Light says something different.
Light calls it unconditional love—
loving without control,
caring without collapse.

Your Lamp shines intentional light on the guardrails in your life—
not to block your road,
but to protect you from cliffs
and dangerous turns.

## Rest as Fuel

Sometimes my body says, "Sleep."
And my mind says, "Not yet."

I've learned that voice is often ego and conditioning—
trained by a world that is fast, loud, and never satisfied.

This world demands motion
without caring if the well is empty.

It praises speed
without checking the fuel gauge.

A body that isn't filled will stall—
maybe not today,
but soon.

"Hurry up," the world says.
"Get there."

But I've hurried before.
And ended up nowhere.

More times than I like to admit.

There was a night I ignored my tiredness.
I told myself I could go a little farther.
I waited too long to pull over.

And when I finally had to stop, my options were bad ones—
loud groups, unsafe places, nothing that felt right.

I stayed awake until daylight.
Then I moved on to somewhere safe.

Nothing happened.
But it could have.

The real mistake wasn't the night.
It was ignoring what I already knew.

I was too tired to listen to my own good advice.

After that, I respected tiredness as information.
Not weakness.
Not laziness.

Rest isn't something you earn after you break.
It's something you use so you don't.

## Calm as Strength

When I was younger, I worked in a hospital.
I learned the lesson of calm every single day.

Calm makes room for good decisions in a crisis.
Calm saves lives.

And sometimes, later in life,
we have to relearn that same lesson—
not in emergencies,
but in our own living.

## Presence as Medicine

Presence is what calm looks like in action.

Sometimes all it takes is being there—
listening,
holding a hand,
not trying to fix anything.

Presence eases fear.
Presence softens anxiety.

It lights the soul
and reminds us we are never alone.

In the hospital, one of the first lessons in healing was simple:
distraction.
Not denial—redirection.

A story.
A question.
A hand to hold.
A window to look through.

Fear loosens its grip when the mind is invited somewhere else.

Your mind cannot hold two full thoughts at once.
It cannot stay trapped in fear
while being gently led into comfort.

Distraction isn't avoidance.
It's a reset—
a doorway out of panic
and back into the moment.

## Lighting Without Burning Out

Burnout is real.
And it shows up when boundaries are ignored
and the fuel tank is never filled.

You can't keep helping if you are empty.

Everyone eventually learns what they need
when burnout is circling.
That's when you give yourself permission to reset.

Maybe it's a five-minute walk.
Maybe it's meditation.
Maybe it's changing the subject to something gentle.

One doctor once told me,
"Hug a tree. Walk barefoot in the grass."

Connect to something bigger than yourself.

However you do it—
what matters is that you do.

# Walking Away Without Going Dark

I have walked away before.
In the beginning, it was in the dark.

Now I walk away with knowing.
With clarity.

I understand my boundaries.
I honor them.

I know my direction.
And I know the road I choose to travel.

# Becoming What You Needed

I have no doubt now that I have been becoming exactly what I needed to become—
right when I needed it.

We've talked about the why
and the how of this journey.

It grows into Intentional Light—
the practice of becoming a Lamp Lighter
for yourself
and for others.

And as Napoleon Hill said,
"Every day and in every way,
I get better and better."

# CLOSING — CARRYING THE LIGHT FORWARD

## You Don't Save the World

I was never motivated by saving the world.
That always felt grandiose—
more like ego than truth.

What matters to me is quieter than that.

A moment of peace.
A moment of confidence.
A moment of hope.

That's enough for a life well lived.

## You Tend the Flame

In all my experiences along this path,
my answer always comes back to the same place—
awareness.

You tend the Flame by keeping yourself,
and your thoughts,
in the Light.

By noticing what you think.
By questioning what you believe.
By choosing clarity when confusion is easier.

Awareness is the hand that shields the Flame
so it doesn't go out in the wind.

# Others Find You by It

Like a moth to a flame,
we are all drawn to Light—
even when we are new to the journey.

The path grows familiar.
Sometimes we walk it with others.
Sometimes we walk it alone.

Some will follow.
Some will lead.
Some will choose roads already worn smooth by many feet.

And still,
each of us must decide
which road is truly ours.

# Acknowledgments

I honor my life and all its twists and turns—
every experience,
the joyful ones and the painful ones,
that turned me in directions I never planned.

What once felt like tragedy
became the doorway to peace and happiness.

I couldn't see it then.
And maybe you can't see it yet.

My hope is that you find your Intentional Light
and become a Lamp Lighter
in your own life.

# About the Author

I'm not here to save the world.
I'm here to live my life honestly—and light my own way while I do it. My life has taken turns I never planned. Some were beautiful. Some were devastating. All of them shaped me. What once felt like tragedy became the doorway to peace, strength, and clarity—but I couldn't see that at the time. I just kept walking.

For nearly a decade, I traveled alone across this country. The road taught me who I was when there were no familiar maps, no roles to perform, and no one to lean on but myself. It taught me awareness. It taught me courage. It taught me how to listen—to fear when it warned me, and to intuition when it guided me.

That journey led me to what I now call **Intentional Light**—the practice of choosing awareness, clarity, and inner authority. Not loudly. Not perfectly. But deliberately.

I believe:

Calm saves lives—sometimes literally, always inwardly.
Boundaries are not walls; they are guardrails.
Rest is wisdom.
Awareness is power.
And light is something you tend, not something you wait for.

I write for the woman who is walking her own road—sometimes with others, sometimes alone—trying to trust herself, understand herself, and choose her next step with clarity.

I don't promise easy answers.
I offer lived ones.

If my words help you feel steadier, braver, or more at home in yourself—
then that is more than enough for me.

Jo Landolfo

www.ingramcontent.com/pod-product-compliance
Lightning Source LLC
LaVergne TN
LVHW090537110826
845146LV00003B/1145

* 9 7 9 8 9 9 4 3 8 5 8 3 8 *